Merie Blundell

LINDFIELD

in Watercolour

Dedication

To the memory of Bob
for his love and inspiration

First published in 2007 by S B Publications
Tel. 01323 893498
Email: *sbpublications@tiscali.co.uk*
Web: *www.sbpublications.co.uk*

ISBN 978-1-85770-332-0

Designed and edited by Andy Thomas, Vital Signs Publishing. Email: *info@vitalsignspublishing.co.uk*

KING
EDWARD
HALL

Acknowledgments

I have researched the brief histories from many sources, including two excellent books; Helena Hall's *Lindfield Past and Present*, which my husband gave to me when we moved here forty years ago, and Gwyn E Mansfield's *Within Living Memory*.

Contents

Foreword

My husband and I came to Lindfield over forty years ago to look at houses. We parked in the car park on Lindfield Common and I knew this was where I wished to live.

Many visitors used to come into The Birman Gallery when I was working there, and said they had stopped on the way to the coast to have a look around our lovely village. They would ask if there was any literature with a brief history of the village and it sowed the seed that maybe one day I could produce such a book with my paintings. I hope I have achieved this and that you will enjoy this book.

Merie Blundell

1. The Clock House
2. Thatched Cottage
3. Old Place
4. Kempes Studio
5. Pretty Corner
6. All Saints Church
7. The Tiger
8. The Bower House
9. Froyls
10. The Viking
11. The Bent Arms
12. Malling Priory
13. Barnsland & The Well House
14. The Red Lion
15. Humphreys Bakery
16. The Toll House
17. The United Reformed Church
18. The Old Forge
19. King Edward Hall
20. The Pond

P - Parking
T - Toilets

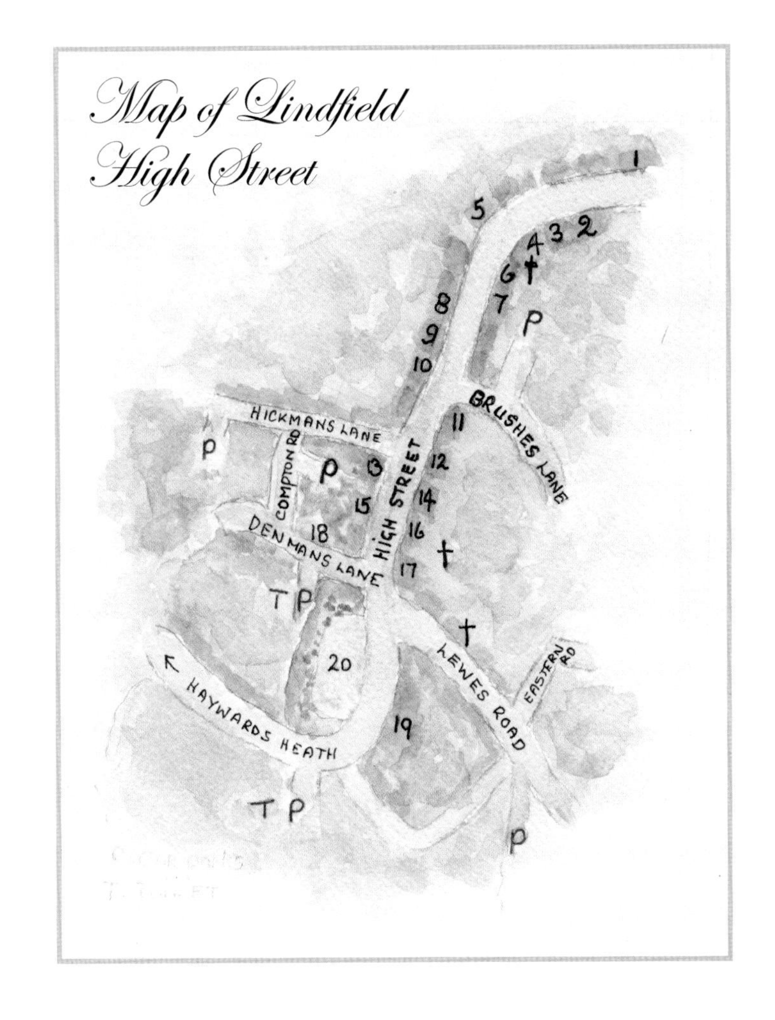

Village For All Seasons

As winter fades gently away
Spring arrives with a bright new day
Colours galore adorn the street
And crocuses spring beneath our feet
The trees do stir and yawn
Heralding the bright new dawn
And weeks of colour we behold
Before summer comes so hot and bold
Window boxes with colour so profuse
Appear in every corner one can use

Autumn creeps in with colours so mellow
Gently bringing orange, brown and yellow
The cooler winds begin to bawl
And drops of rain begin to fall
And then everything turns to white
With snow such a beautiful sight
With hope and luck it might prevail
A Christmas so white and pale
To dust the houses with its magic wand
And back to olden times we will land

Lindfield

It matters not when one visits Lindfield because, as the title of the poem states, it is a village for all seasons.

Spring is lively, with the lime trees springing into life with their buds and the colourful crocuses in the grass verges.

Summer is peaceful, with the sun reflecting back from the windows and time to have lunch or tea in the many public houses or tea shops.

Autumn is beautiful, with the lovely soft gold shades of the foliage settling down for sleep during winter.

Now winter, especially if we have snow at Christmas, is a jolly season, with all the brightly lit gift shops and galleries, the toys in the toy shop eagerly awaiting the young faces to peer through the window in anticipation and hope for the Christmas to come.

Lindfield was previously Lindefelda - 'open land with lime trees' - in a Saxon charter of 765 AD, and stands above the upper reaches of the River Ouse. King Edward III granted the town a Royal Charter to hold a market every Thursday and two annual eight-day fairs.

The High Street follows a track that has many listed buildings, some of which are from the 12th century. Lindfield was a thriving and prosperous village and very important for its industrial activities, producing paper, string, candles, gloves, gaitors, etc.

Hickmans Lane was originally named Hackmans Lane and there were two toll gates - one still exists as The Toll House today. The two 'turnpike' gates shut and a toll was charged for opening them for traffic. The money was kept for the upkeep of the road.

England's toll gates were officially dismantled between 1827 and 1872, but Lindfield's were not removed until 1884.

The Clock House

Approaching Lindfield on the road from Ardingly, we first come to The Clock House on the right hand side. It stands on the corner of Spring Lane and was originally called Spring Cottage. Over the years it has been renovated internally in keeping with its original character.

The previous owners, Roger and Christine Newman, found a well of clear water underneath the floorboards while decorating one of the downstairs rooms. It had been boarded over and was obviously a well originally outside the cottage, which had been built upon.

It is believed there is a smugglers tunnel nearby, from Spring Lane leading to the church.

Thatched Cottage

This cottage is believed to have been the first home of the Chaloner family before they built Old Place in 1590. It is also thought to have been the hunting lodge of King Henry VII. It is now a private residence.

Old Place

Old Place was once the Tudor manor house of the Chaloner family and is one of the most beautiful timbered buildings of its period in all Sussex.

The beautiful gates leading to Old Place were made by John Sharman, who worked at the Smithy in Denmans Lane for sixty years.

Charles Kempe, the famous Victorian architect and stained glass artist, moved here from Brighton in 1875. Examples of his work can be seen in Lindfield Church, including the chancel screen. He loved entertaining, and decorated Old Place inside and out. The main entrance and east wing contain some of Kempe's finest interiors and have since been divided into separate apartments.

Charles Kempe's wooden studio can be seen in the grounds of Old Place in a watercolour on page 19.

Kempe's Studio

Charles Eamer Kempe was a famous local architect and stained glass artist, as described on page 16. Examples of his work can be be seen in Lindfield Church, in the ceiling to the nave. It also contains two examples of stained glass in the style of the Kempe Studio bearing his badge - a sheaf of corn.

Pretty Corner

What more beautiful approach could you ask for on entering Lindfield than Pretty Corner, so well named?

The two houses here were built in the 16th and 17th centuries and have changed very little over the years.

All Saints Church

The first recorded date for this church is 1230, but its origin goes back much further. Its name has changed several times over the years - St John the Baptist, St Peter, St Margaret and St James are all mentioned in local records. The dedication of All Saints came many centuries later.

The ceiling to the nave is the work of local architect Charles Eamer Kempe, (see pages 16 and 18). It has fine examples of stained glass in the style of the Kempe studio.

The war memorial in the churchyard was designed by Sir Ninian Comper.

The Tiger

The Tiger is one of the oldest houses in Lindfield and was probably built by the Canons of South Malling. From 1461 a family of merchant adventurers named Michelbourne lived here. Edward Michelbourne was knighted by Robert Earl of Essex. The family crest was a tiger and Sir Edward called his ship *The Tiger*.

Large homes in the 14th and 15th centuries always kept open house and gave hospitality to travellers. They were the origin of the public houses today.

As few people could read, the Michelbournes used the tiger as their sign, so the house has been called The Tiger ever since. When the family left Lindfield, their home became a public house and inn. The Tiger is now the official church house.

The Bower House

The Bower House is an early timber framed house built at the beginning of 1300 when Edward III was king. The front was rebuilt sometime in 1725. In the past it was fashionable to have a house refronted to disguise its true age.

Other houses refronted were Froyls, Seckhams, Everyndens and The Manor House.

The lane between The Bower House and The Welkin leads to The Vicarage, bought in 1939 and home to successive vicars.

Froyls

The first record of Froyls is from 1706 when it was sold to Dr Henry Tuppen, whose son Dr Richard Tuppen inherited it in 1806.

Richard Tuppen was a great friend of author Charles Dickens, who was often seen walking to and from church when staying at Froyls. Dickens frequently visited Lindfield and may have given readings in the village Assembly Rooms. Dickens also helped raise funds to build the school on the common - now turned into flats. He gave £100 to the vicar, Mr Sewell, to help restore the church, though Dickens often fell asleep during his extremely long Sunday sermons! When awake, he sometimes made sketches of the congregation.

Froyls is one of the houses refronted to hide the Elizabethan building behind.

The Bent Arms

In earlier days this inn was known as Wichelo's and later as The White Lion. The sign was originally the crest of the Bent Family, the original owners. In 1920 a bad fire would have wrecked the whole building but for the prompt attention of the Lindfield Fire Brigade. When it was restored, the first floor ceilings were raised and a new attic floor built.

The rooms below belonged to a carriage builder, Julius Guy, who made gigs there until he died in 1913, aged 82.

Viking Cottage

Viking Cottage was originally named Secomb's Cottage, and at the end of the 19th century gloves were made there. It is believed many of the very stout beams all over the house came from old ships. The building fell into disrepair after the death of Mr Bish, the owner, and was purchased by a London lady, Mrs Blight, who renamed it Viking after the famous Captain Blight's ship.

After she left around 1934, it was purchased by a Miss Bassano, who turned it into a library from where she would drive around to outlying parishes which had no library of their own. When World War II began, Viking Cottage became a private residence again.

Adjoining Viking Cottage is Chantry Cottage.

Malling Priory

Malling Priory, built in 1370, is best seen approaching from Hickmans Lane. It was once also known as Cheaters and Taylors and it was not until the Wilson family occupied it that it reverted to its original name of Malling Priory.

It is an impressive Georgian house and has some unusual window and door configurations. It was once the home of John Bent, whose brewery extended from Malling Priory to The Bent Arms. Alongside is Malling Cottage and Priory Cottage, which were once three small houses. Nearby is Crosskeys, built in the same period. Malling Cottage has old beams in every room, dating from the 15th century.

In the front wall of Malling Priory there is one blocked out window, reminding us of the unpopular window tax, which was not abolished until 1851.

Barnslands and Well House

This is one of the most picturesque houses in the High Street. The gable end and timber probably dates back to the 15th century.

About eighty years ago the Holman family lived in the northern cottage with a greengrocery business. Later, a Mr Crossley also ran a greengrocery business, which had a lovely colourful display of fruit and vegetables from the house to the pavement. Mr Holman kept cows in the shed at the rear of Barnsland, now called The Barn, and he used to take his cows to the common and bring them back in the evening. They were often seen in the pond!

A Miss Savill eventually bought the house when it fell into disrepair, restoring it into two houses. The thatched barn at the end of the garden she also made into a charming cottage.

The Red Lion

Over 200 years ago, an inn was established on land known as Paynes Tenement. In 1790, approximately three coaches a week travelled through Lindfield and Ditchling on their way to and from Brighton, calling at The Bent Arms and the inn which would become known as The Red Lion around 1823. (Confusingly, Porters next door was also called The Red Lion until 1720.)

The new Red Lion became particularly favoured as it had a spacious yard for changing horses. Travelling by coach was very hazardous in those days.

The Red Lion is a fine building in the middle of the High Street, preserved as being of architectural and historic interest.

RED LION
RED LION

Humphrey's Bakery

The bakery, established since 1796, is set in the cross wing of an early medieval hall. A receipt, in latin, dated 20th August 1453 for rent paid to the rector, was found behind a beam while it was being repainted in 1947.

A special baking tin was kept for the church's sacramental loaves and not used for any other purpose. Later, wafers replaced the bread.

In 1895, Mr Mead the baker retired and his assistant Richard Humphrey became proprietor, since which time the business has been known as Humphrey's Bakery. Richard Humphrey was the baker for fifty-five years and died aged 85.

The Toll House

The Toll House dates from 1630, and in modern years until recently it was an exclusive clothes shop.

The toll gates across the road at The Toll House were removed with great ceremony in 1884, when villagers gathered for the removal and The Red Lion held a celebration dinner in the evening. The wood from the gates was saved for a Guy Fawkes bonfire on November 5th.

The United Reformed Church

Built in 1857-58, this church replaced a chapel built in 1811.

The adjacent house, Rycroft, was purchased in 1888 as a manse (a home provided for the church minister), but was later sold in 1953 as its upkeep proved too expensive. It was then repurchased in 1975. A new hall was added in 1959 and further enlarged in 1996.

The Old Forge

John Sharman was a blacksmith and he worked in Denmans Lane at the forge for over sixty years.

The old Sussex custom of 'firing the anvil' on St Clements day to frighten off evil spirits was revived by Mr Sharman for the celebration of the 'relief of Mafeking' at the Queen's coronation in 1953. The relief of Mafeking occurred on 16th May 1900 when the army arrived to relieve the garrison at Mafeking, South Africa, where Colonel Robert Baden Powell - with just 1500 troops - had held out against 7500 Boers.

When he retired, the smithy continued in business under George Brown and then Bill Bartley. In 1984 the building was modernised for retail purposes.

King Edward Hall

The village hall was named after King Edward VII, who visited Lindfield a few months before his death in 1910.

In 1887, Dr Daunt, who lived in Pierpoint House near The Tiger, tried to secure a public hall as a jubilee memorial to Queen Victoria, but his scheme was dropped, being unpopular at the time. The present hall was opened for social activities on 17th January 1911 and has proved very popular ever since.

In the First World War the hall was used as a hospital, and in the Second it was used for military lectures and physical training. The Lindfield Players put on plays for soldiers and other people devoting proceeds to charities.

The architect of the hall, Mr Tower, gave his services for free and also donated the billiard table to the Mens' Club. Mr Sturdy of Paxhill gave the site, part of which was formerly the garden of the delightfully named Pear Tree House.

Lindfield Pond

This is a natural spring-fed pond and is home to many fish, ducks and often swans. Over the last few years, even a heron has visited Lindfield pond.

There used to be ramps on each side where, in the 19th century, Mr Holman the farmer brought his cows here in the afternoons. The right-hand side is now a favourite seating area.

The pond has been painted by many artists and is a great attraction and feature of the village.

Lindfield Common

At the end of the High Street we come to Lindfield Pond, King Edward Hall and Lindfield Common, which is host to many celebrations and festivities during the year. There are tennis courts and a pavilion for cricket in the summer and a field for football and many other sports in the winter.

There is a village day in June, which starts with a colourful parade. Floats begin from Hickmans Lane playing field and end on the common where schools, sports clubs and charities all have stalls, selling plants, cakes, toys, etc. There is also fancy dress and many competitions, including sports events and lots of entertainments ending with the 'firing of the anvil' (see page 46). It is a happy day for all ages.

On November 5th, Lindfield Bonfire Society organise a wonderful display of fireworks with a huge bonfire built by villagers beforehand. The proceedings start with a colourful procession from Hickmans Lane playing field. The High Street is closed to traffic during the parade.

Epilogue

Opposite, and on the last page, are a few of the other interesting features and signs around the village.

As we come to the end of this book, I hope you have enjoyed it as much as I have painting and writing it.

Merie Blundell, 2007

LINDFIELD
Best Kept Village
in all
SUSSEX
1993-1994
1995

KING
EDWARD
HALL

RED LION

LINDFIELD